UNPLUG

BREATHE

CREATE

A MONTH OF
REDISCOVERING YOUR
CREATIVE CONFIDENCE
THROUGH MEDITATION

www.inomniaparatuspublishing.com

"CREATIVITY IS SEEING WHAT OTHERS SEE & THINKING WHAT NO ONE ELSE HAS THOUGHT."

—ALBERT EINSTEIN

This journal is part of the UNPLUG BREATHE CREATE series & designed to be used alongside a bespoke guided meditation.

Download this month's meditation using the QR code below:

HOW TO BEST USE THIS JOURNAL & MEDITATION

UNPLUG

The first step to reconnecting with ourselves as creative beings is to unplug & disconnect even temporarily from the countless electronic tethers that keep us firmly held in the world of shoulds & must's.

BREATHE

Take a few deep breaths, paying close attention to the way oxygen moves through your mouth & nose, filling your lungs & reawakening the creative genius locked safely within you, exhaling any fears, hesitations, or doubts that may filter your magic.

CREATE

Release your desire to control, plan & perfect every step & movement you make. Embrace the often wild, messy & chaotic magic that comes with allowing your inner creative to explore & play. Prepare yourself to experience fulfillment & satisfaction in new & creative ways.

DAILY ROUTINE

While moving through your day, begin implementing the use of affirmations. Both habits & beliefs are formed & strengthened through consistent repetition & before you know it your thoughts will become truths.

Included below are powerful affirmations that when paired with your daily tasks & activities, will empower you through this month of finding & claiming your own creative space.

I recommend repeating one or more of these affirmations aloud anytime you find yourself in front of a mirror, washing your hands, or refilling your beverage of choice.

I AM CREATIVE.

I AM CONFIDENT.

I AM AN INSPIRATION.

30-DAY ENERGY TRACKER

When you've completed your daily meditation, make note of a single word or phrase that best describes your energy level in that moment.

Day 1	Day 2	Day 3	Day 4	Day 5
Day 6	Day 7	Day 8	Day 9	Day 10
Day 11	Day 12	Day 13	Day 14	Day 15
Day 16	Day 17	Day 18	Day 19	Day 20
Day 21	Day 22	Day 23	Day 24	Day 25
Day 26	Day 27	Day 28	Day 29	Day 30

DAY 1

What was the last compliment you received regarding your creativity? How did it make you feel? How can you bring more of that feeling into your daily life?

ON A SCALE OF 1-5 WHAT'S YOUR
CURRENT CREATIVITY LEVEL?

DAY 2

What resistance or fears do you feel around the idea of expressing your creativity with confidence? Are these feelings based on facts or assumptions?

ON A SCALE OF 1-5 WHAT'S YOUR
CURRENT CREATIVITY LEVEL?

DAY 3

Imagine it's 30 days in the future, and you're confidently expressing your creative genius every Write a letter to present-you from your future self.

_____

_____

_____

_____

_____

_____

_____

_____

_____

_____

_____

_____

_____

_____

_____

_____

_____

ON A SCALE OF 1-5 WHAT'S YOUR
CURRENT CREATIVITY LEVEL?

DAY 4

When do you feel most creatively confident? This may be when you're playing with words, music, paint, food, dance, clay, wood, steel, yarn, etc. Describe how you feel.

....

....

....

....

....

....

....

....

....

....

....

....

....

....

....

....

_____

_____

_____

_____

_____

_____

_____

_____

_____

_____

_____

_____

_____

_____

_____

_____

ON A SCALE OF 1-5 WHAT'S YOUR CURRENT CREATIVITY LEVEL?

DAY 5

How did you most enjoy expressing yourself creatively as a child? Is that something you might still enjoy today?

_____
_____
_____
_____
_____
_____
_____
_____
_____
_____
_____
_____
_____
_____
_____
_____
_____

ON A SCALE OF 1-5 WHAT'S YOUR
CURRENT CREATIVITY LEVEL?

DAY 6

What does creative confidence mean to you? How are you embodying being creatively confident in your daily life? How can you embrace this more?

_____

_____

_____

_____

_____

_____

_____

_____

_____

_____

_____

_____

_____

_____

_____

_____

_____

ON A SCALE OF 1-5 WHAT'S YOUR
CURRENT CREATIVITY LEVEL?

DAY 7

Do you consider yourself to be intuitively creative? If so, how does this manifest in your life? If not, how might you explore what it means to trust your intuition in regard to creative expression?

ON A SCALE OF 1-5 WHAT'S YOUR
CURRENT CREATIVITY LEVEL?

DAY 8

What's one creative practice you could confidently teach or share with others? Is this something you've done in the past? If so, how did it feel? If not, how might you explore sharing your skill with others?

ON A SCALE OF 1-5 WHAT'S YOUR
CURRENT CREATIVITY LEVEL?

DAY 9

How confident are you when it comes to writing creatively? Is this a practice you enjoy, something you'd like to explore, or an idea that leaves you feeling anxious?

_____

_____

_____

_____

_____

_____

_____

_____

_____

_____

_____

_____

_____

_____

_____

_____

ON A SCALE OF 1-5 WHAT'S YOUR
CURRENT CREATIVITY LEVEL?

DAY 10

Close your eyes. Take 3 deep breaths & ask yourself,
how do I want to explore my creativity today? What
answer do you receive? How comfortable are you with
trusting your intuition to guide your creativity?

ON A SCALE OF 1-5 WHAT'S YOUR
CURRENT CREATIVITY LEVEL?

DAY 11

When was the last time you created something for fun, without purpose or direction? How confident did you feel? What did you enjoy most about the process? What hesitations did you experience?

ON A SCALE OF 1-5 WHAT'S YOUR
CURRENT CREATIVITY LEVEL?

DAY 12

Do you have a journal, notebook, or whiteboard where you can capture your sparks of creative genius? If so, how often do you revisit these ideas? If not, take this time to create one.

ON A SCALE OF 1-5 WHAT'S YOUR
CURRENT CREATIVITY LEVEL?

DAY 13

Today's prompt is a little different. Set a timer for 5 minutes & doodle in each of the areas below, something that fits the shape of the space. When time is up, look back at your creations & make note of any themes. Perhaps there's a bigger project hidden within one of your tiny bits of creative genius.

ON A SCALE OF 1-5 WHAT'S YOUR
CURRENT CREATIVITY LEVEL?

DAY 14

What is one task that you complete every day. This may be something mundane, administrative & without much sparkle. How can you approach this task from a more creative standpoint?

ON A SCALE OF 1-5 WHAT'S YOUR
CURRENT CREATIVITY LEVEL?

DAY 15

How can you weave more creativity, confidence & joy into your daily life? Perhaps it's dancing while cleaning house, wearing silly socks, or replacing the words, 'I think' with 'I know,' for an entire day.

ON A SCALE OF 1-5 WHAT'S YOUR
CURRENT CREATIVITY LEVEL?

DAY 16

Failure is a part of life, it's also part of the creative process. When did you last fail during a creative project? Focus on the fact that while the outcome may have fallen short of your intention, it was temporary & there is no reason to not try again.

ON A SCALE OF 1-5 WHAT'S YOUR
CURRENT CREATIVITY LEVEL?

DAY 17

How often do you allow yourself to embrace your own creativity? What's holding you back from prioritizing this time? As with any habit or skill, consistent repetition strengthens & solidifies your confidence as a creative being. Are you able to set aside 10, 20, or even 30 minutes each day to explore your creativity?

ON A SCALE OF 1-5 WHAT'S YOUR
CURRENT CREATIVITY LEVEL?

DAY 18

Who are some of your creative role models? What is it about them that inspires you? How are you similar to these role models? Do you believe these traits were learned or something they were born with?

_____

_____

_____

_____

_____

_____

_____

_____

_____

_____

_____

_____

_____

_____

_____

_____

ON A SCALE OF 1-5 WHAT'S YOUR
CURRENT CREATIVITY LEVEL?

DAY 19

What sounds, smells, colors, temperatures, or environments most ignite your creative confidence? Do you have a specific soundtrack you like to listen to, or a candle you light?

ON A SCALE OF 1-5 WHAT'S YOUR
CURRENT CREATIVITY LEVEL?

DAY 20

How do you currently include creativity in your work or career? How might you be able to include more?

_____
_____
_____
_____
_____
_____
_____
_____
_____
_____
_____
_____
_____
_____
_____
_____

ON A SCALE OF 1-5 WHAT'S YOUR
CURRENT CREATIVITY LEVEL?

DAY 21

Through the meditation, you hear your higher self speaking to you from within your reflection. What things does your higher self have to share with you?

ON A SCALE OF 1-5 WHAT'S YOUR
CURRENT CREATIVITY LEVEL?

DAY 22

How do you best communicate your creative side? Is it with words, actions, music, service, food, or something else? Is this something you explore regularly? Why or why not?

ON A SCALE OF 1-5 WHAT'S YOUR
CURRENT CREATIVITY LEVEL?

DAY 23

Where do you feel the most resistance when it comes to embracing your own creativity? Are these feelings based in past experiences or assumptions?

ON A SCALE OF 1-5 WHAT'S YOUR
CURRENT CREATIVITY LEVEL?

DAY 24

When do you feel the most creatively confident?

_____

_____

_____

_____

_____

_____

_____

_____

_____

_____

_____

_____

_____

_____

_____

_____

ON A SCALE OF 1-5 WHAT'S YOUR
CURRENT CREATIVITY LEVEL?

DAY 25

What forms of creative expression do you find come most easily, naturally, to you? When do remember first being aware of this ease? How might you apply these same feelings to new forms of creative expression?

_____

_____

_____

_____

_____

_____

_____

_____

_____

_____

_____

_____

_____

_____

_____

_____

_____

ON A SCALE OF 1-5 WHAT'S YOUR
CURRENT CREATIVITY LEVEL?

DAY 26

How would you choose to creatively express yourself today, if time & money weren't factors? What's holding you back from doing so? Is it truly time, money, a fear of failure, or something else?

_____

_____

_____

_____

_____

_____

_____

_____

_____

_____

_____

_____

_____

_____

_____

_____

ON A SCALE OF 1-5 WHAT'S YOUR
CURRENT CREATIVITY LEVEL?

DAY 27

How are you currently communicating your unique voice, message, or story to others? How might you be able to bring more creativity into this process? What feelings or hesitations do you feel around this?

ON A SCALE OF 1-5 WHAT'S YOUR
CURRENT CREATIVITY LEVEL?

DAY 28

As children, we're naturally curious & willing to try new things, getting creative even when it may be uncomfortable. How can you embrace your childlike curiosity & creativity now?

ON A SCALE OF 1-5 WHAT'S YOUR
CURRENT CREATIVITY LEVEL?

DAY 29

Oftentimes the key to building creative confidence is maintaining a beginner's mindset, remaining open & curious to the countless solutions surrounding us. How can you better embrace a beginners mindset?

ON A SCALE OF 1-5 WHAT'S YOUR
CURRENT CREATIVITY LEVEL?

DAY 30

When do you feel most creatively confident? Where in your body do you feel this? How would you describe this feeling or sensation? How might you be able to weave this into your daily life?

_____

_____

_____

_____

_____

_____

_____

_____

_____

_____

_____

_____

_____

_____

_____

_____

ON A SCALE OF 1-5 WHAT'S YOUR
CURRENT CREATIVITY LEVEL?

If you already have an UNPLUG BREATHE CREATE subscription, keep an eye on your mailbox for your next delivery.

If you aren't yet a member but would like to be, or are interested in gifting a membership to someone else, scan the QR code below.